THE THIN WHITE LINE

THE THIN WHITE LINE

BY

RYAN W. DANIELS

NPP Books
http://www.nppbooks.com

The Thin White Line.

Publisher: NPP Books, 15 Sunset Road, Arlington, MA, 02474, U.S.A.

Printed on Demand in the United States of America and United Kingdom.

First Edition

International Book Standard Number (ISBN): 978-0-916182-20-5
(Hardcover, 244 x 170 mm, Pinched Crown, Case Laminate)

To: My family and especially my loving wife Shaobei, who has patiently endured through all my work, and has always served as a great source of love, inspiration, and hope to me.

I would also like to thank all the editors, illustrators and photographers who helped to make this book possible, not to mention all my fellow ex-pat bicyclists who shared the dangers and joys of bicycling on the city streets in that wondrous country...China.

Photographers: Baoling Huang, Duan Zhou, Ru Chen, Xiaoming Li

Cover Photo: Daryl Luk

Illustrations: Mike Overbeck

Editors: Kenneth Domino, Johanna Seelan

CONTENTS

PROLOGUE

The asphalt blurs beneath me, all but hypnotizing me. My legs continue to pump up and down, like some old reliable steam engine propelling me forward. I see the shoe first, an old battered square toed leather one of the kind favored by the men in China. I always thought they looked rather like a shoe worn by the Pilgrims, minus the buckle of course.

It sat there upright, as if the owner had taken it off and placed it there. I slowed my pace, my bicycle's brakes squeaked in protest. The other black leather shoe passed by, but this one was flipped over. Unlike its cleaner brother, a lot of hardened mud clung to the underside of it.

The bicycle was relatively intact. The front wheel (轮子, lun zi) was certainly finished, bent like a pretzel. The basket (篮子, lan zi) was crushed and nearly torn from its holdings. Old bluish paint covered the frame. Weather and time had had its way with this bike, as the paint was chipping off and covered with rust. The company logo was still faintly visible. The road wheels were bald, the treads gone from years of use. "Baloney tires" my grandfather used to call them. Stuffing was poking out from the seat, its hard covering cracked from age.

While this old bicycle lay in front of me in mock agony. I couldn't help but wonder how the rider must be faring. He was obviously a man, I could tell that from his shoes. But how old? Married or single? Handsome or ugly? Serious or carefree? Maybe his carefree nature is what caused the accident. I can make little sense out of the clues left here, this usually the case with most accident aftermaths that I stumble across.

I come to a full stop. My boots touch the pavement. I fold my arms across the handlebars and coolly survey the scene in front of me. On average I see it about once a week. It's always there, constantly reminding you of your own frailty.

His groceries lay scattered across the pavement. Tomatoes, lettuce, Tofu, a carton of milk. The milk is leaking, making a small white river leading to a larger white pool about the size of a fist. A slightly larger pool of red is next to the white, as if daring it to come over and join it. "A bottle of white, a bottle of red" song comes into my mind briefly. Needless to say this one had been a bad one.

By now a sizable crowd of onlookers has showed up. The Chinese are a race of watchers; they love to watch the comings and goings of the world. But they prefer to stand on the edge of the picture. This time they have come to see the body, except there isn't one; there never is. The state cleanup crews do their jobs exceedingly well. In a few minutes they will hose away the two pools, one white the other red. The bicycle will be picked up by a scrap dealer, and the groceries, shoes, swept away. Then life will resume as usual, like nothing ever happened here. Because it's all too upsetting, we don't like to be reminded that he/she could be next. As I pedal away, I wonder if I will be.

人行道

FORWARD

I have lived in Hangzhou, China for five years. I have come to know much of her people, culture, and language in that time. Many things about this country amaze me. I've had my share of both pleasant and unpleasant surprises. It might appear at times that I am looking down on the Chinese people; this is certainly not the case! I am simply stating facts, things I have witnessed with my own eyes and know to be true. I can furthermore say that I have a special love for this country and her people. Living with them for so long a time has made them my family; although I know that I can never truly be one of them. Finally I don't pretend to know everything there is to know about China and bicycles. This work is taken from my own experiences; I hope the experts who read this will forgive my ignorance in certain areas.

INTRODUCTION

China. This one word conjures up images of a Great Wall, a populous people, Buddhist temples, a serene bamboo forest, and a very difficult language among other things. For me, China was and still is all these things. However, all the travel books I read could not prepare me for what I encountered during my stay there. I'm sure most of you readers, having read the John Doe rides across "random country" by bicycle genre of books. In and of themselves, they are fine and interesting books; however this book is not one of them.

This book covers the short cross city travel that most of you adventurers will encounter upon your stay in China. Be you a business person, English teacher, or student, you will take part to some extent in the gritty daily commutes in the cities of China. The favored vehicle of choice: the bicycle, as it is relatively cheap, reliable, small, and suitable for the short distances covered in a city. Buses are all very well, but notoriously crowded, and you go where the bus goes, not much freedom to explore. Cars are good when leaving the city, but get used to being stuck in traffic; also finding a parking space is getting more and more difficult. This is because by and large the cities of China were not designed to handle so many cars. They are also expensive and you must obtain an international driver's license. Taxis are good, but are expensive if you operate on a shoe-string budget as do most travelers. It also helps if you speak good Chinese, because most of the taxi drivers will not speak much English. Walking is reliable to say the least, but most of the cities are quite extensive, and a little more speed is required to get around, which leaves us with the bicycle.

The bicycle was adopted by the majority of the Chinese people in the mid-20th century; it was cheap and easily mass-produced in the state-run factories. Upon visiting mainland China, one can see hordes of people moving down the bicycle lanes, all going about their daily business. Many bikes can be seen, old ones ready to fall apart, brand new ones with shock absorbers, ones with three wheels, even the new electric bicycles that run by battery. Second only to the diversity of the bikes, are the riders themselves.

In China it is not uncommon to see a businessman, complete with a suit, tie, and briefcase, riding alongside a migrant worker covered in mud. You see mothers and fathers bringing their little ones to school, the kids riding on the newspaper racks behind them. Or you'll see a gas delivery man; balancing four propane tanks slung two to a side on his bike. He very carefully balances while he rides, sometimes leaning to one side, to compensate for the absence of a tank. Mixed in with this group are hundreds of China's college elite. Students ride casually; with girlfriends riding sidesaddle across the back of their bikes, all the while happily chatting away on their mobile phones, usually keeping one eye on the road.

With all this activity going on in the bicycle lane, not to mention the rest of the road; an accident is only a matter of time. Someone is not paying attention at the wrong moment, or talking on their mobile phone; perhaps he/she is in a hurry and decides to run that red light. Then the worst happens. Traffic accidents are very common in most countries, China not being the exception. Yet, China has more people than many other countries put together. So when all these people decide to move around at the same time; draw your own conclusions.

Roughly 100,000 people die each year in China from traffic related accidents. That's not counting the maimed and injured. Hangzhou, my city, has many dead each week, from traffic related accidents, according to local news sources.

I found it rather laughable that my students were absolutely terrified of getting SARS in the spring of 2003. I told them that they had a much greater chance of getting into a traffic accident than dying from SARS; still, they seemed rather unconvinced. Perhaps it's because we feel powerless; we have no control over diseases. Most people are afraid to fly, even though it's been proven the safest way to travel. They are afraid because they have no control over the airplane. We feel in control when we drive a car. In reality, it's a false sense of control. You have no 100% safety guarantee when you head out for the day.

Riding a bicycle here in China is no exception to this rule. It looks dangerous upon your first inspection of the streets; I won't lie, it sometimes is. It takes a little courage and self-confidence to get on that bike and to go out and join the commute. If this is not for you, then now is the time to put this book back where you found it.

But, if you are willing to step out of your comfort zone, as I'm sure most travelers are, then exploring China's streets by bike is an experience that will be difficult to match. I've intended this book to be a companion for a larger and more comprehensive travel book on China. As I will not discuss the more cultural issues of the Chinese people, I will try and stick to my own experiences in the bicycle lanes of Hangzhou.

These lessons and experiences can be applied to any large city in China. I want to convey to you, the reader, tips, tricks, experiences, accidents, lessons learned, and common sense: things that I had to learn for myself upon my arrival and prolonged stay in China. My aim is to educate you in the ways of the bicycle.

Hopefully after reading this, you will have a better understanding of the cityscape in modern China, as well as the rules of the road there, and you will be able to more safely enjoy your stay, while exploring the streets and back alleys in the cities of this great country.

CHAPTER 1

"WHAT YOU'RE GETTING INTO"

When riding a bicycle (自行车, zi xing che) in China, there are a thousand little dangers, as well as delights. The cities have modernized rapidly; so as to give the tourist a view of the "new" and "old" China. A rider can see some traditional Chinese homes with white mud walls and black tile roofs. But after going a mere 20 feet you view a brand new skyscraper, one that would rival anything in downtown New York City or Tokyo.

As a result of China's economic boom, more people here are able to buy cars. This is good for them, not so good for you, though! Most of the proud new owners of cars in China have minimal driving experience.

The Chinese RMV does not operate the same as its western counterparts. Corruption and bribery are common ways for many drivers to get their licenses.

The bicycle lanes are your friend, stay in them. That is the first thing you should know, although the lanes sometimes have a way of disappearing, leaving you in the middle of the street, or mysteriously morphing into a passing lane, breakdown lane, parking lane, taxi lane, runway, etc. The streets in China's cities are more friendly to cyclists, having large bike lanes (as I shall refer to them) which are about the width of a car and a half. Picture a breakdown lane, there you go, a bike lane.

Most readers would agree that it is only natural to stay out of traffic, or to look both ways before crossing the street. I myself have done some stupid stunts on my bicycle here, which would have made my mother very upset. So yes, after the bike lane, the second rule is common sense. But still, please stay in the damn bike lane.

Sometimes the bike lanes will be enclosed and protected from traffic. Most of the time there is just a thin white line separating you from traffic. Within this lane you will share your daily commute with as diverse a group of people as any country could boast.

Many are kind and considerate, others rude and aggressive. Some pay no attention to their surroundings, appearing to be mesmerized by something up ahead. Still, more just push ahead lazily, apparently in no hurry whatsoever. Their speed is neither fast nor slow; I suspect most of these commuters travel this speed to safely avoid collisions. Or should the collision occur, to minimize the impact damage.

Earlier I mentioned a thousand little delights, as well as dangers. Most people like to hear the bad news first. So as for dangers, there are many. Ranging from something as trivial as a flat tire, to something as catastrophic as being hit by a bus or truck. This is of course a worst case scenario and seldom happens, but it still happens. The former happens with much greater frequency. About bicycle maintenance I will go into greater detail later on, but it sometimes seems like a full time job, due to some street conditions, or the general wear and tear on your bike.

Ah, the 1,000 delights of riding a bicycle through the cities of China. Now with the bad news past, I can share with you the good news; Riding across China's cities gives you an unmatched sense of mobility and freedom of movement, one that you couldn't achieve with a bus or even a car.

While you ride, feel free to explore the back alleys or "hutongs". Here you will experience the "real China". It gives the adventurous rider a real treat to see the Chinese going about their daily business. Mothers or even grandmothers carrying little infants on their backs, Children, all dressed in school uniform, complete with pioneer red neckerchiefs, skipping happily without a care in the world. Or glide silently past a small grocery store where the shopkeeper wonders if he really just saw a foreigner go by? Perhaps it was his imagination, he thinks while he continues with his work.

Your bicycle jumps and bucks underneath you, similar in fashion to a rodeo horse. The ground gets steadily worse, going from concrete to loose gravel.

You pedal across an ancient arched bridge. You can't help but wonder if some long gone emperor had walked across this very bridge. You enjoy the inertia while going down as curious migrant workers pause in their destruction of an old apartment building. One of them shouts "Hollo"! The only English he knows. Deftly skirting around some bricks and crumbled mortar from the site, you continue on.

Now the road begins to improve. The bicycle lane reappears and becomes separate from the traffic lane. A nice low-cut hedge separates you from the cars; on the right side is the sidewalk, numerous shops and stores.

You pass Pedi-cabs, which slowly plod along with some talkative students in the back seat (座椅, zuo yi). The driver is standing while he pedals, trying to get up some speed. You are happy that you don't have this job as your bike is much quicker and more agile. No sooner have you finished this thought than an E-bike zooms past. A well-to-do Chinese woman dressed in business clothes, swears harshly in Chinese as a taxi comes into the lane and almost hits both of you.

Applying the brakes, you slow down, as the taxi continues on its mad dash up the bicycle lane; almost hitting several other riders. "That was too close," you think to yourself. A traditional Chinese market is near your home. On passing you must slow down due to all the pedestrian traffic. Ducks hang on meat hooks; rows of all kinds of vegetables line the stalls. Fish, turtles, frogs and eels are sold in another corner.

The smell here is sweet, the smell is terrible, the smell is stale, and it's unnamable. Whatever it is you only get a brief whiff of it. The next smell to assail your nostrils is the reek of diesel oil, and engine exhaust. The bus in front of you rumbles to a slow stop. A faintly lit #42 appears on the digital display on the rear window. Dust has coated the windows and turned the white paint grey. You dare not pass it on the right side, as passengers are getting off and on. The left side is preferable even though you are vulnerable to traffic. Passing the bus you coast into your apartment complex. You politely get off your bike and walk it past the grey uniformed security guards, who suspiciously look you over, or smile brightly, mostly depending on their mood. After riding into the bicycle garage, you dismount, flipping down the kickstand, and making sure that all the locks are securely in place. You head for your apartment, and congratulate yourself on another safe ride home.

The above is a sample of what a foreigner can expect during one of his/her daily commutes in the cities of China. At times it can seem confusing, even chaotic; while it can also be a wonderful way to view the Chinese and their culture. Seeing and experiencing things that the ordinary tourist could not.

Whatever your reason for staying in China, once you mount a bicycle and join the Chinese commuters in the city streets, you undergo a change. It's rather difficult to describe. You cease to be a green tourist, you are still a foreigner, and nothing changes that. But you become more street savvy, perhaps understanding the Chinese character a little bit better: and you appreciate your long forgotten friend from childhood....the bicycle.

CHAPTER 2

"CHOOSING A BICYCLE"

The bicycle is one of an ex-pat's best friends while living in China. It's also a useful helper to a tourist or traveler with an intended short stay, so when choosing your bicycle, don't make any hasty decisions. Take your time and shop around; as prices vary according to the type of bike. This chapter is intended to help get you started, to help you find a reasonably priced bicycle, with the necessary fittings, as well as some tips and more tricks of the trade to keep your bicycle for as long as possible.

Walking down a typical city street in China, you have an abundance of choices for bicycle shops, everything from the new department stores, to the small "mom and pop" shops, all trying to outdo one another. It is good for the traveler to take advantage of this competitiveness. I would recommend that you try the large department stores first. I say this because the quality of the bikes there is usually good, and the salespeople very helpful. But, that's not to say the small stores are bad, some of my friends have gotten very reliable bikes there at great prices.

Before I continue, I must admit I felt like a 10 year old boy again, when I strolled between the rows and rows of sparkling, new bicycles, it was a very nostalgic feeling; Running my hand over the sleek metal of the handlebars, or playfully ringing the bells (铃, ling). Listening to see which one I liked the best.

It was surely a blast from the past. I hope the reader will have a similar feeling the first time.

The most important thing is to choose a bicycle that best suits your lifestyle in China. Consider your everyday situation. Do you have a long commute to work? Do you just want to ride around and see the sights? Will you want a bicycle that will help you carry your groceries home; or perhaps all of these. There are usually four main kinds of bicycles to choose from: the mountain bike, 10 speed, E-bike, and the common single gear. I will discuss all of these in brief detail. It's up to you to choose which one will best suit your needs.

The Mountain Type Bike:

This one is my personal favorite. The one word I would choose to describe this bike would be "Durable". The construction of this kind of bike is usually very strong, and also low maintenance; which is good if you are a novice rider in China.   I can't tell you how many times I have ridden over trash, bricks, holes, or been clipped by other rider, only to have my bike keep going.

The thick tread tires are perfect for the debris strewed areas of the city and resistant against nails or sharp stones which would penetrate a normal city tread tire.   The newer models possess shock absorbers which make the ride much more comfortable.   All in all, the mountain bike is a good all around workhorse for your stay in China.

The 10 Speed:

The key word here is "Speed". If you are the kind of person who needs to get places in a hurry, then this type of bike is for you. However, it sacrifices durability and ruggedness for its speed. It is also difficult to carry things on this bicycle. It should also be noted that replacement parts are a little more expensive and sometimes harder to come by than for the other types of bike.

Common Single Gear:

By far this is the most common bicycle used by the Chinese people, and with good reason of course. It is cheap, reliable, easy to repair (修车, xiu che), and unremarkable. If bicycling is not a joy to you, and you simply see it as a means to an end, and you don't want to spend much, then this bicycle type is what you want. Most go for under $30.00 US, so you can't go wrong. Should you have the misfortune of it being stolen, then no big deal. They are easy and cheap to replace.

While some of the other types of bicycles have limitations concerning baskets, the single gear can be outfitted with any manner of them. You will recognize the usefulness of this once you have spent a week in China. The only downside to this bike is that it tends to break quite often, and you could slowly be spending more than you bargained for just to keep it running.

The E-Bike:

This one is the new kid on the block, and judging from the number of them on the streets, the most popular. The E-Bike or Electric Bicycle is powered by a large re-chargeable battery. This battery propels the bicycle along, with speeds reaching up to 25 miles per hour! The E-bike also possesses pedals as backup if the battery is low.

There are many advantages to this type of bike. If you want to get somewhere quick, with no physical exertion, while carrying things or people, this bike beats out all the others. This would explain its immediate popularity in the cities of China. The main drawback of the E-bike is the very thing that makes it a success: the battery. If the battery dies when you are out in the city, you will be pedaling back home. While the E-bike is fast and agile with the battery at full charge, without it the bike is very heavy and cumbersome. The pedals are awkward to use. I've seen low-powered E-bikes limping home, while children's bicycles shoot past them.

Town Bikes and Rentals:

The city of Hangzhou, Zhejiang province where this book takes place, has recently implemented a new system of bike usage for the public. I recommend this if you are a traveler passing through the city and buying a bike would not be practical; Or if you are staying for a period of under six months. The day rental is quite a bargain, which you might have to do when renting one! However, it's an unforgettable experience to ride around the Famous West Lake and take in the sights and sounds with the freedom of not being tied to a tour group.

The town bikes are a new innovation recently implemented by the government in Hangzhou. These bikes are dispersed around the city in various locations, where they are locked in place by a security system. To access them you must first put a deposit of 200 RMB, then have your bus card charged. Then simply go to a location with the bikes, tap your card on the podium, a beeping sound should emit forth, and then the bicycle will be unlocked. The first hour is free, the second costs you one RMB, and the third is two RMB and so forth.

The good news is that you can reach just about any location in Hangzhou within one hour of riding. I sometimes found it difficult to locate one of the bike stations in order to return the bike, and got charged a little extra. Also it pays to feel the bikes' tires and check seat heights, before you scan your card. You don't want to get stuck with a bicycle that is too small for you, or has flat tires. But for the most part they are a really convenient way to get around the city. The last I heard, many cities in China were beginning to adopt this system.

Hopefully, by now you are ready to choose your bicycle. Whatever bike you choose, I would recommend a dull-colored one. I say this because, the duller your bicycle looks, the less attention it will attract, hence the less chance a thief (小偷, xiao tou) will notice it. Also on a final note for this section, the gender of the bicycle does not matter in China. In my hometown I would be laughed off the street for riding a girl's bicycle. But here, no one seems to notice. I've seen some tough construction workers riding pink polka dotted girls bicycles, and nobody cares. So don't worry about such things during your stay.

Accessories:

Accessories are important to your bicycle. Would you head out the door to work without your glasses, watch, and wallet? No, of course not. The same goes for the accessories for a bicycle; I refer to them as locks and the "3 B's" or Bells, Brakes, Baskets.

A bell is important. If you can't speak Chinese, then how else do you expect to tell someone you are coming up fast on them? Bells are cheap, usually costing about one US dollar, and well worth the price I might add. Sometimes they are ineffective as most people in China's cities have grown up hearing them, and become desensitized to the noise. This leads me into the most important accessory.

Brakes. Not the kind you take at work. But the kind that stop you from hitting that taxi that shoots around the corner. I can't begin to tell you how important a good set of brakes are. Most of the brakes that the stores equip the bikes with are adequate. Just make sure they are really tight. The brake cables will loosen after a few weeks, but it's easy to have them tightened by a street shop.

A basket is a necessity as well. It only takes one trip to the supermarket to realize how convenient it is to have a basket. It's quite a feat to balance one's groceries on both handlebars while navigating through crowded, traffic choked streets. There are several different kinds of baskets from which to choose. By far the most common one is set in front of the handlebars. I would recommend this one, as it's easy to look after what your carrying. Other types include "folders", metal collapsing baskets which hang off the newspaper rack on your bicycle's rear sides, similar in idea to saddlebags. They can be conveniently folded flat against the frame when not in use. Still others can be placed atop the newspaper rack; as you will see there are countless variations you can come up with concerning baskets; Now, on to one more important accessory, the lock.

Locks will be the only thing separating your bicycle from being snatched in a heartbeat. Naturally, you will want to choose a good, strong, sturdy lock. Or better yet, I would suggest that you should purchase two. Start with the rigid "D" lock and add a flexible lock later. The latter prove their usefulness when you have to lock your bike to a tree, lamppost, or even a friend's bicycle. It should be remembered though, that these locks can be picked quite easily by a skilled thief. They are only meant as a deterrent.

Helmets and pads are, of course, a good thing. They might be what saves your brain in a head-on collision with an electrical pole. I will just inform the reader that almost no one wears either helmets or pads while riding in China. The motor scooters require a helmet, by law. But, the bicycles have no rule for this. So be prepared to put up with all the stares and the chuckles of the people as you ride by.

By now you should have your brand new bicycle with all its accessories. I'm sure you're just dying to head out and explore the wondrous city you have taken up residence in. We will look at your first time out in the next chapter.

CHAPTER 3

"HEADING OUT"

I recall my own first time on a bicycle in China. I looked at the traffic and was scared to death. I hadn't been on a bicycle since I was 16 years old! I think the key on that first day, was simply getting some practice in before I headed out into mainstream traffic.

Most likely you will be living in a university or similar enclosed establishment. Before you hit the open streets, I suggest riding around on the relatively traffic free campus roads. This way you will get the feel of your bike, how well it corners, how quickly it can stop. After you feel comfortable with this, by all means go out and explore the city. Just remember to take it slow and try to keep your eyes on the road at all times.

Now there will be a lot of interesting things to look at. In fact before you know it your head will be looking in all directions except straight ahead. China's cities are perhaps some of the most fascinating areas of the world! From my own experience I almost had about five head on collisions, because I was busy looking at everything. After a while you will get a sixth sense of what is around you. I will go into this later in the book, though.

China is modernizing very rapidly. Hence, her cities are changing virtually overnight. This can make orientation interesting, especially if you have an out of date map, say six-months-old or so. You will find that some streets don't exist anymore; squares disappear, apartment blocks take their place, etc.

Maps are, of course, useful, but it's also a good idea to make use of very old and relatively new landmarks. The higher and more noticeable the building and hill, the better. It might seem childish, but trust me; getting lost in a country where you don't speak the language is a real headache.

I mapped the whole of the city of Hangzhou out in my head. I did this by simply going around one block at a time. Then after this you can begin to memorize all the small alleys and hutongs, which are a real treat to explore. After a few months who knows? You may be leading your Chinese friends around in their own city! Some other things to consider, perhaps you should bring some sunscreen and a hat. Water or juice is also good to bring along on a hot day, especially in China's southern cities.

Chapter 4

"Know your fellow commuters"

As you've probably noticed on your first day out, there are many different kinds of denizens in the city. The next chapter is devoted to your fellow commuters who share the bicycle lane with you, and may prove themselves to be obstacles in your daily commute.

While you are still getting adjusted to life in the bicycle lane, you will no doubt become aware of its residents, who fall into many different categories due to their certain types of behavior while riding. This chapter has been devoted to them; so that you might navigate safely through them.

Believe it or not, there is a pecking order on China's streets. From buses and trucks down to small children's bicycles, everyone knows their place. You'll need to learn the system so you can navigate safely through...

Trucks/Buses: The undisputed lions of the road. Always be sure to yield when you are next to them.

Taxis: Crazy in any country, China's taxis' are no exception. Watch them carefully. They tend to swing into the bicycle lane without warning if they see someone in need of a ride.

"Trashmaster 5000": A motorized version of a "San lun che", these rickety trikes will take you around the city, if the price is right. Recently they have been banned in some major cities.

San lun che: A 3-wheeled, all-purpose carrier. These trikes are the workhorses of the under classes. You will undoubtedly see many variations, from sanitation carts to rickshaws. They can be found in any city in China. They are mostly slow and bulky.

E-bikes: Or Electric bicycles, one step up from a common bicycle. Battery powered, they zip around the bike lanes. They are difficult to hear until they are right next to you.

Rider Personalities:

Duals: One rider with two bikes. Perhaps he is just helping a friend out, or delivering an extra bike somewhere. Be cautious when you pass by, as his balance could be upset very easily.

Cell-phoners: You are familiar with the phrase "hang up and drive"? In this case it should be "hang up and pedal". As in most countries with mobile phones, this is a big problem on the street. These folks are oblivious to what's happening around them.

Baby on board: These bicycles are equipped with children's seats mounted on the newspaper racks. Usually the only danger they pose is if you are distracted by the cute smiling faces of the children.

Lover's Lift: When a wife or girlfriend hitches a ride on a bicycle not built for two. The woman rides sidesaddle across the back. Under Chinese law this is illegal. So is stealing, but it happens.

Walkers: Whether out for a stroll, J-walking, or whatever, they have a habit of getting in your way. Since you are on a bike and they are on foot, you will come up on them extremely fast. Your mind will sometimes play tricks on you as they are head level with bikes, and you think they are on bikes and you can scream past them. I almost had several collisions with people walking in the bike lanes, so be wary.

Knowing these different types of commuters will help you later on. Here I've only touched on it briefly. I will discuss it in much more depth in chapter 7.

CHAPTER 5

"TRICKS OF THE TRADE"

During your stay in China, your bicycle will need repairs from time to time, whether it be something as simple as putting more air into your tires or as complex as changing an axle. This chapter will deal with little maintenance concerns such as how to jerry rig baskets and other accessories to your bike. I hope these little tidbits prove useful to you while you traverse the city.

Now let us suppose that you are riding your bicycle along and all of a sudden....POP! Your tire has gone flat. You dismount, and upon closer inspection you find a nail embedded in your tire. This is a fairly common occurrence in the cities of China, due largely to all the construction going on. Needless to say, you should find a bicycle repair shop to fix it; I would recommend walking your bicycle while you search for one. However, if it is the front tire, it is still possible to ride. Be warned, though, that you will have very little ability to steer and maneuver, which is of the utmost importance on the busy streets here.

If your back tire took the hit, then I'm afraid you're walking, as riding might damage the bicycle further and end up costing you more money to fix. Finding the bicycle repair shops is sometimes easier said than done. There are many, but they are difficult to see as they seldom have large signs announcing their presence. They always seem to be sandwiched between small "mom and pop" stores, or noodle restaurants. The sidewalk in front of the repair shop will usually be a darker color due to all the oil (油, you) stains from several years and thousands of bicycles being serviced. Upon closer inspection one will also notice all the spare parts lying around or hanging on the walls of the same dwelling.

Language is usually not a problem with the bicycle repair men. Most likely they don't speak English, but they can understand what's wrong with your bike. Pantomiming is also a highly entertaining way for you to get your point across, both for the repairman and you.

Gesturing became so much a part of my daily routine in China that I continued to do so upon my return to the United States. I remember telling my mother that someone had called for her, while holding my hand up to my ear in the shape of a telephone; she thanked me with a raised eyebrow.

In order to help you, I'll include some useful phrases and words to make your bicycle repair stop easier. A punctured tire is usually going to cost you about 3-4 RMB. (Subject to change).

Jerry Rigging

In addition to the repair shops, you can always rely on yourself. If you happen to be a jack of all trades, or fancy yourself a handyman, by all means take your bike apart. Jerry rigging is very common, and I would encourage it. You might even learn a lot about yourself when you repair something haphazardly; Such as how ingenious you can be. Duck tape and wire are the jerry rigger's best friends; also, I recommend buying a small cheap tool kit. I can't tell you how many times I've used it to fix or tighten something on my bike; or how many times my ex-pat neighbors used it to do the same.

The first things to break on most bicycles are the mud guards or fenders. They tend to be an easy fix, although most people I knew just simply threw them away after they broke. Personally, I find great value in fenders, to protect the tops of your tires, but mostly to keep the rainwater back-splash off your clothes.

It largely depends on where you choose to reside in China, but you will find yourself out in the rain sooner or later.

One trick for staying dry that I learned from watching the Chinese cyclists, is to put a plastic bag over your bicycle seat. This serves to keep the seat dry and, more importantly, your rear end. You will also see many of the Chinese with plastic bags tied around their shoes. As every experienced cyclist knows, your feet are the first parts of your body to get soaked. Yes, it looks silly, but it will save your nice hush puppies from water damage.

Distressing or Camouflage

Bicycle thievery is a big problem in the cities of China. It also doesn't help that you are a foreigner and, in most cases, stick out like a sore thumb. The bike thieves being ever vigilant will snatch your nice new shiny bike the second your back is turned.

How do we avoid this scenario? Well, there is no 100% guarantee that your bike will not get nicked. I lived five years in China and had two bikes stolen; that's a pretty good track record, by the way. One English girl I knew had two bicycles stolen in just under a month! If you talk with some ex-pats who have lived in China, everyone seems to have a bike-theft story, which brings us back to the point of how to cut down your chances of becoming a statistic.

First follow these simple guidelines:

1) Distress your bicycle. Buy a can of spray paint, preferably grey, brown, black, any dark dull color will do. Spray the frame, cover over anything shiny. The duller and more inconspicuous your bike looks, the better.

2)   Leave ample time for the paint to dry. When dry, find a large mud puddle, toss bike into said puddle. Let dry again for two hours. Then should the urge take you, throw several stones at your bike, scratch the paint a little, and continue until desired aging is achieved.

3)   Buy two locks. Locks are relatively inexpensive. I recommend buying a "D" lock, which you can attach to a holder on the frame, and when used is fixed between the rear tire and central frame. The other lock is the longer flexible cable lock. These ones can be used to lock your bike to a pole, tire, friend's bike, etc. When not in use, I store this one around my handlebars. (Make sure to paint these as well, as they are usually very shiny neon rubber over a steel cable.)

4)   Use caution and a bit of paranoia when parking your bike somewhere. Find a place that you can easily observe through a store or restaurant window. If in a restaurant, sit accordingly, if a store, you might want to check on your bike every now and again.

Please remember that these are just words of caution, largely drawn from my own experiences. It is my firm belief that they do cut down the chances of your bicycle being stolen. Many shopping malls will have security guards to watch the bikes. Try to keep your bike parked as close to the buildings as possible. The thieves typically go for the bikes that are parked right next to the street. Safe areas would be the apartment complexes or the colleges that you reside in, as they are walled compounds with bike stowage sheds.

Identification:

Another minor dilemma I've had was coming out of the grocery store to gaze upon a sea of parked bicycles, and wondering, "Dude, where's my bike"? Mercifully, you won't have an annoying little sidekick to repeat that catch line. It's all up to you to identify your bike; they are issued with small license plates. But the last thing you need to remember when moving to a new country is your bicycle license plate number. I suggest scratching a symbol into the frame somewhere, or covering your seat with a certain type of plastic bag. These suggestions will also help you to prove its your bike should it get stolen then found again.

Stowage:

If your bicycle is your main mode of transportation, then you will definitely want to utilize every available square inch of space. I took great joy in devising new ways to carry more things on my bicycle, everything from groceries to small tools for quick repairs, as well as a place to attach a rain poncho.

As for carrying boxes, groceries, other odds and ends; Space is at a premium on your bike. You can find an abundance of attachments and upgrades at every store that has bicycles. Buying a basket for the front of the bicycle is a good move. Normally they can hold two small bags of groceries; in addition to this they make good bumpers, I remember that it was my basket that saved me from getting a facial from the back of a truck that stopped abruptly in front of me. The basket slowed the impact, and my face stopped about 3 inches from the truck's fender.   Then I got off my bike and pushed the basket back into shape. Good as new!

Saddle baskets are also very useful; I bought one for the right side of my bike. This increases the range that you can travel, buy something and bring it back comfortably to your apartment. Then after use, simply collapse the baskets, and you have a few extra inches to maneuver in traffic.

The E-bike's seats open up to reveal a nice stowage area, not very big but quite secure. Most of them also come with a little stowage bin on the rear of the bike. It's alright for keeping a raincoat in, but little else will fit in there.

Rust is your worst enemy, but also an unlikely friend, because it helps in camouflaging your bike. It eats your baskets, in some cases in only a matter of weeks. I recommend checking the quality of your baskets before making a purchase. On a final note, don't forget the importance of the bicycle bell. It has helped me to avoid innumerable collisions, granted many people ignore it, mostly because they are used to hearing it. Still it's an important and essential part of your bicycle, don't forget to pick on up!

Now you should be ready to head out on the crowded streets. Although you will not always be in good weather in your commutes, this next chapter touches upon the skills you will need to ride in adverse weather conditions.

CHAPTER 6

"NIGHT AND ADVERSE WEATHER RIDING"

China's weather is like that of any other large country possessing many different climates-from cold sub-zero steppes in Manchuria, to tropical steam baths in Guangdong province. The weather varies quite a bit from place to place. Hangzhou, the city where I resided, has a sub tropical climate; making the biking relatively easy year-round. One of my friends, who lived in Beijing, found it very difficult to bike during the wintertime due to all the snow and ice. Where-ever you decide to settle in for your expat experience is largely up to you. There are some basic guidelines and knowledge you should know regarding....

RAIN

When it rains it pours, goes the popular saying; this is true in many parts of southern China. Tropical downpours were a new experience for this New England Yankee. I remember being out on my bike cruising around the city. The sun was out, looked like a great pleasant day.   Then (you know what's going to happen next, don't you?) the storm clouds gathered, and within the space of five minutes, I was a very wet and shivering Yankee.

I adapted quickly enough, though, learning that the next thing to buy after your bicycle is a rain coat or "poncho" as we like to say. Buy the rubberized ones (20 RMB), they are more expensive than the plastic ones, but the quality makes it worth the extra cost.

Little things I learned about the rain poncho. (I call them ponchos because they have no sleeves and a space for your head to go through) They have a hood, which is great for keeping the rain off, but it severely limits your peripheral vision, which proves key to your survival on a bike in the cities. The hood also muffles sounds while you are riding, so two of your most important senses are handicapped in the rain. Just be extra careful and aware of this.

Concerning clothespins

"Clothespins" Wow, there's a word I've not heard in a long time, thanks to dryers everywhere. Well, the clothespin is still very much alive and well in China; and becomes very useful when it rains. While wearing your poncho and slowly riding along in the rain, it's customary and good sense to drape the front of your poncho over the basket. This serves to protect whatever you're carrying from the elements, also to keep two to three inches of water out of your lap! It's sometimes windy and your poncho cape will flap over your shoulder exposing your groceries. What to do? Enter the clothespin. Just drape your poncho cape over the rim of the basket and attach the clothespin, a good strong wooden one will do. If you are still unsure of how this works, look at all your fellow commuters, they will be more than happy to provide an example..

Umbrellas

I also recommend that you pick up an umbrella before you do much travelling around your city. Buy a small collapsible one; these are easy to stow on your rear newspaper rack. The ponchos are great for keeping the rain off of you during your ride, But you really don't want to walk around in them when they are wet, as the water sluices down them and onto your knees, soaking your pants.

It's all about having the right piece of equipment for each task; the poncho to get you there, the umbrella when you are walking around. Also remember NOT to leave your poncho with your bike; chances are someone will steal it before the rain ends. Many riders in China prefer to use the umbrella when they ride down the street. While this is a quick fix to avoid being soaked, it's quite dangerous to your fellow commuters as umbrellas can block your vision, the vision of those around you, can poke you in the eye, etc. Should a strong gust of wind hit, you will become Mary Poppins in the blink of an eye!

Wet brakes/ muffled bells

Much like your car back home, the bicycle's brakes get wet and you lose a crucial second or two of stop time while pressing them. While riding in the rain, apply pressure on your brakes every now and again, especially when approaching a busy area, or going down a hill. There is a big difference between wet and dry brakes, and you can feel it.

One more thing about ponchos and bike bells; when you have the poncho on and clipped to the front of your bike, the sound of the bell is muffled significantly. So instead of cursing, "Why can't these people hear me?!" just pull back your poncho, so the bell can be heard.

Night Riding

China's cities have an amazing night life to offer. Restaurants that are open all night long, shows, malls, karaoke bars, ex-pat pubs. The list goes on and on. While you are out enjoying yourself, bear in mind that eventually you will have to head home, preferably before the sun comes up.

Riding your bike at nighttime is quite different than riding during the day. It can be more dangerous due to your vision being reduced. Often, though, I find it a very pleasant experience. For one thing, there are not as many people out, as in the day. Another thing you have going for you is the streets are normally very well lit. The only time you will have to contend with pitch black streets is in the side alleys or underpasses. In that case, slow down, keep your ears/eyes peeled and proceed with caution.

There are many dangers facing your ride home in the dark, but by far the most common is road debris; Concrete chunks and bricks that had fallen off dump trucks during the day. Being rather small, these obstacles are easily hidden by the inner city gloom until it's almost too late, only a last-second swerve would be enough to save you.

Every ex-pat pretty much has some story about how they, or someone they knew, narrowly avoided or didn't, some road debris. It's actually just a formality during your bicycling career in China. You just get used to it, but never get complacent about it, always be on your guard.

One more thing about "night obstacles"; watch out for missing storm drain covers! The scrap dealers get top dollar for them. Some unscrupulous individuals will go and steal them under cover of darkness. This leaves you with a huge black hole that will swallow your front tire, and put in you the Olympic freefall competition. To avoid such a fate, I humbly recommend that you ride your bike as close to the center of the bike lane as possible.

Other Considerations

As in the day time, some people prefer to ride the wrong way on the bicycle lane. They will come at you very quickly, so you need to see them a good distance off. Most of the bicycles in China don't have headlights. The E-bikes do, but they are also moving at a very high speed.

Another nighttime phenomena I experienced, and I never mentioned this to other ex-pats, so I don't know if they experienced it either-was a strange sensation of being overtaken by another rider, when it turns out that it was only my shadow overtaking me. This was due to the high powered street lamps. It still served to spook me, as I assumed the other mystery rider was so close as to collide with me. I promptly swerved to the right to avoid sure disaster, and then realized I was all alone in the bike lane. The next street lamp came and then I realized what I had seen. It still would continue to spook me from time to time. I think I was just getting paranoid at that point.

Dust Storms

To those of you brave adventurers who aim to take up residence in Beijing or similar other northeastern cities in China, be ready to ride through an occasional dust storm. Yes, that's right, sand storms or I will call them dust storms.

Most westerners think of China as a land of lush bamboo thickets and tropical jungles. This is true, but China also possesses deserts, mountains, icy windswept steppes, tundra, and temperate climes. Many of China's deserts are advancing, wanting to take up residence in the cities. The important thing to know is that you will have to ride through a dust storm sooner or later, so it's best to be prepared.

I have a confession to make. I've never ridden through a dust storm. As my city was subtropical, I have no experience in this. But because I care about you, the reader, I want you to be ready for anything, so one very hot dry day, I rode behind some dump trucks that were kicking up huge billows of fine dust. It was unpleasant to say the least. Based on this experiment I came to several conclusions.

1) Dust or dirt in your mouth has a rather chalky and gritty texture, makes it difficult to swallow and is generally unpleasant. I would wear a mask or bandana to cover your mouth.

2) Your vision is greatly reduced, take it real slow. Protect your eyes: rider's goggles would be a good investment.

3) Dust causes minor wear and tear in the gears/chain (链条, lian tiao) on your bike. Oil and dust don't mix.

Snow

This is a major impediment to all cyclists, as anyone who has grown up in a cold climate will tell you. I only had one instance in Hangzhou when it snowed. It snowed about one or two inches, roads iced up, bicycle travel became treacherous. I remember riding my bicycle to English class. The bicycle lane was bordered by a hedge on one side and the sidewalk on the other; there was a thin layer of black ice beneath the snow. One after another a few Chinese riders began to lose control of their bikes, and then tumbled to the ground. The furthest one, Thump! The second closest one, BAM! The closest one, KAPOW! I stopped, or so I thought, I couldn't stop. My bike was sliding, and you get that one panicky second where you know you're toast, and there's not a thing you can do to save yourself. My bike slide out from under me sideways, THUNK! It's of the utmost importance to remember; in the 1.5 seconds it takes you to hit the ground, always put your arms around your head! Protect your noggin at all costs! Everyone who had fallen seemed to be okay. My fall had hurt, but I survived relatively intact, and I had learned a valuable lesson: in the snow, bikes are about as useful as a pair of ice skates in the desert.

It is a lot to remember for novice riders who are just getting their feet wet, but after a time it will become second nature when you ride. More often than not you will hook up with some friends who have been in-country for awhile. I'm sure they will show you the ropes.

Next I want to share with you the essential experience of the gritty street. I'm talking about the high noon showdown of you vs. the whole city. Your commute will take you through some hair-raising twists and turns, near-misses, frustrating waits, moments of the strange and sometimes absurd, and also some of the most memorable and exciting times during your stay in China. Throughout the Earth, this time is called rush hour. I prefer to call it "The ballet of Chaos".

CHAPTER 7

"BALLET OF CHAOS"

The ballet begins 7-9:30am and again between 3:30-4:00pm and goes through 6pm. The sheer amount of people and vehicles of every size and description is mind boggling! Millions of people all trying to get home after work and school. It's truly an unforgettable experience.

Due to my overactive imagination, I always had a fantasy; that usually happens when I'm at an overcrowded intersection in China. All the bikes are lined up at the edge of the intersection, people and bikes are intermingled scarcely inches apart; cars and taxis, buses and trucks all revving their engines, waiting for the lights to change. Then the light changes, or you hear a shrill whistle and everyone surges forward in a seemly unstoppable human/machine tide, sweeping all before it.

During these moments I would often imagine myself "going over the top" as they did in WWI, also to the sound of a shrill whistle. One moment all was quiet and orderly, the next, noisy and chaotic. Or one could liken this experience to the scene in the movie "Brave heart" where the Scottish lines charge forth. There are many other examples that I'm sure you can draw from your own imaginations.

This is rush hour in China, and you are stuck smack dab in the middle of it. The first thing I would recommend is that you not panic. Always go with the flow of traffic, never against. This might even mean you will get swept a little bit off your intended course.

Many of the drivers in China are still novices. Just a short 20 years ago, cars were still something an average family could only dream of having. Now the city streets are flooded with them. And they make life very difficult for the bicyclist. Most of the cars are manual stick shifts, the drivers frequently miss the gears and stall out; and this proves troublesome when you are right behind them keeping pace. One thing I recommend is to watch the drivers through the rear windshield, as their movements might give you some insight as to what they are about to do, or not do. This sounds silly but I lived by it for more than five years and it saved my neck numerous times. So give it a try. This strategy also works with other bike riders who are ahead of you.

Comrades in Commute

I would like to touch upon your fellow commuters in this chapter and the best ways to deal with them. There is a long and varied list, and undoubtedly you will find many new types of commuters in your sorties about the city.

Buses

Buses are the undisputed lions of the city streets. They are bigger than you; therefore they have the right of way. As you will no doubt notice, there is a "pecking order" on the streets of China. It's best to find your place and stay out of the bigger guys' ways.

My experience with buses is that while they are big, they are relatively slow. They have a tendency to sneak up behind you when stopping for passengers. You are riding quietly along and then you glance casually over your shoulder, and AH! A bus barely a foot from your rear tire, how about that?!

When you are on the other end of the bus, and it stops to pick up passengers, always go around it on the side facing the street, as passengers will be getting on and off. You never want to get sandwiched between a bus and the curb. Buses can also be used to your advantage. When turning or crossing at intersections, buses make great shields. Just keep pace with them, and shadow their movements until you have crossed the danger area. Nobody is going to broadside a bus with their car! They might try it if it's just you racing across the intersection, though.

Trucks

Second only to the supremacy of the bus, is the common dump truck. These vehicles are often painted blue or an aqua blue. They rush from construction site to landfill and back again, all the while banging, clanging, and screeching. Frequently you can hear them change gears about a block away, upon hearing this I always chuckle to myself, "If you can't find 'em, grind 'em".

The major dangers these trucks pose to you, besides driving too quickly, is debris falling off the top and projections from the sides of the trucks themselves.

The tops are not secured sometimes, so if one of these highway heavyweights hits a pothole, some of the load might spill out.

Some of the trucks also have metal hooks on the sides. These are for tying down a tarp to cover the load. I have noted that the hooks are just the right height to snag on someone's clothes. I've never actually seen such a terrible scenario played out, but I just wanted for you to be aware of the possibility.

Happy Birthday Truck

Or that's the moniker that I have given to them, interesting story behind that name. One hot dusty summer day, early into my China experience. I was riding along, and I began to hear a faint melody. A little further on, I recognized it as "Happy Birthday to You". It sounded rather tinny as if played over a loudspeaker, then a loud swishing noise kind of like a high pressure water hose. I turned around to see where the sound was coming from when, WHOOSH! I got sprayed by a large jet of water. From the waist down I was soaked!

I pulled over and quickly took a bow for the chuckling citizens, "Exit stage right, I'm a moron, no wait, scratch that, I'm a wet moron." I gazed up the road and saw my tormentor slowly driving away, blaring happy birthday, and spraying down the roads.

These trucks are employed by the city as sanitation vehicles. They are equipped with dual high pressure hoses, which spray down the streets and keep the dust down. How to do this without getting the populace wet? Play a loud melody as you approach to warn them. Personally I always thought it would be great to play the "Imperial March" from Star Wars as you bear down on the hapless populace with high pressure water cannons.

The best way to deal with this occurrence is to learn from the Chinese masters. Upon hearing "Happy Birthday" or some other loud tune and the swishing sound of water, you can time it just right, lift your legs up off the pedals, and only a little bit of your bike will get wet. I watched the Chinese bicyclists put their feet up one after another as the truck came by. You will no doubt master this technique after one or two tries.

Taxis

Yes, I know you were all waiting to read this section. That very word conjures up fear and loathing in forms of craziness across all continents and major cities. Seriously though, taxi drivers are just ordinary Joes, trying to make a living like you and me. I learned most of my Chinese from them; however, I do need to touch upon the role they will play in your daily commute.

Taxis do.....pretty much whatever they want to. That's why you have to be aware of them all the time. These guys have to pay the bills, so if they see someone who needs a ride they will swing right into the bike lane to get them, or the same for dropping someone off. I never got hit but it always scared me when they would zip into the bike lane to pick up/drop off someone.

Riders

Cells "Hang up and pedal!"

Cell phones are the rage among young Chinese. Bad habits are quickly formed with good toys. I'm sure the reader knows all about drivers who use their cell phones. "Hang up and drive!" we scream in frustration.

"Hang up and pedal!" is my personal battle cry upon seeing a youth completely oblivious to imminent danger on all sides, and yet who somehow escapes unscathed!? Yes, I too have used my phone while riding. I would like to say though that I always try to make it a point to pull over and just sit on my bike. It's much safer, trust me, and don't even think about sending a text message while in motion on your bike.

San Lun Che "Trikes"

San lun che's or "Three wheeled vehicles" are the workhorses of the cycling world. They are a common sight on your daily circuit; they can be electric, motorized, or pedaled. I only have a little experience actually riding one around, but I can tell you that they handle like a pig. The break is a lever between your legs that is awkward to use, and it's really challenging to take a corner on them.

Needless to say, you will be seeing many of them. Dodging around them at high speeds becomes somewhat of an art form. The drivers let you know when they are approaching, they shout out something like "Lai Lai!", which means "Clear the way!". I found particular interest in the kinds of loads they were carrying-every conceivable object. From mountains of Styrofoam; to pigs on their way to market, to little kids on their way to school.

When you do decide to overtake a San lun che, treat it in a similar way to overtaking an 18 wheeler truck on the highway. Get behind him, then peek around the side to make sure no one is coming up the wrong way, and when the coast is clear, go for it.

Motorbikes/Scooters

Made famous by names such as "Vespa", these scooters are really just small underpowered motorcycles. I've ridden one once, you can reach speeds of about 40 miles per hour on them. They usually switch back and forth between the bike lane and the traffic lanes as the circumstances suit them. If the bike lane is crowded, they act like a car and take to the proper driving lanes. If there is a lot of traffic they act like a bicycle and crowd into the bike lane. Be wary as the scooter riders sometimes think you are as fast and agile as they.

E-Bikes

To the cycling world in China, E-bikes or "Electric bikes" are the new affordable ride. As discussed earlier, they are a bulky bicycle with stubby pedals and a large battery located between the legs or on a running board.

The main irritation you will have while travelling next to them in the bicycle lane is the awful, hideous, nerve fraying, screeching noise they make when the brakes are applied. You see, the bicycle brakes they have are insufficient to stop the E-bike when it gets up to cruising speed; the result is an awful piercing SCCCRRREEEECCCHHHH!!!! Now, one E-bike making this sound would be bearable, but during rush hour you are listening to dozens of E-bikes. The only remedy I can suggest is using your fingers to plug your ears when at a red light.

As a former E-bike rider and owner, I know that these riders tend to go very fast. I did. The main issue with E-bikes is they are quiet, so difficult to hear when approaching. A couple of times I almost veered over into them, as they had drawn up near me without making much noise. They do make some noise if they hit a bump, all the plastic parts of the bike rattle, betraying their position to you.

Wrong ways

Wrong ways are people who make a bad habit of riding their bikes up the wrong way of a one-way bicycle lane. The danger in this is obvious. I don't know why they do it; perhaps it's an easier way to get to their destination. Maybe they are confused? Who knows!? Even I've done it, for extremely short distances. I don't recommend doing this at all as it's hazardous to your health.

Baby on Board

This is another peculiar area of your commute. I'm sure most people remember seeing those cute, yet slightly annoying, yellow signs, informing all nearby drivers that there is, indeed, a child aboard that Dodge caravan or SUV.

In China, the family Dodge caravan is in actuality a bicycle, motor scooter and or E-bike. It's very common for three or four people to be crammed together onto a motor scooter. Naturally this makes for some dangerous commuting! I find the biggest distraction is when the cute little Chinese baby turns around to look at the wai guo ren (foreigner) who's riding behind or alongside the family.

Spreads and walkers

The last type of commuters I would like to touch upon is of the commonest nature. The "spreads", are what I like to call cyclists who all ride or walk along-side one another, usually three abreast. They are annoying to ride around. They set their own pace and if it's a crowded area, you pretty much just have to ride along behind them.

The "Walkers" are simply pedestrians who feel compelled to walk in the bicycle lane. They can be dangerous, as your mind will play a trick on you, leading you to think that they are on bicycles. They are moving much slower than you, so try to watch out for them. I saw several walkers get hit by bicycles, I remember one poor lady got knocked right off her feet and landed on her back.

Duals

This is one rider with two bikes, Perhaps he is just helping a friend out, or delivering an extra bike somewhere. Be cautious when you pass by, as his balance could be upset very easily. I've also done this once or twice, it's really challenging to hold one bike upright while you try and negotiate the city streets; the key is to go really slow.

Lover's Lift

When a wife or girlfriend hitches a ride on a bicycle not built for two. The woman rides sidesaddle across the back. Under Chinese law this is illegal, but then again so is stealing. If you gentlemen reading this do get a girlfriend over there, then it is best to keep a look out for any police. If they see your girl on the bike, you might get pulled over and fined.

Police and Traffic Assistants

You are probably starting to wonder where the order is in all this chaos?! Where is the thin blue line to hold back the onrushing tide of humanity? They are there to be sure, but in small numbers, and spaced out strategically to maximize their effectiveness.

Traffic cops in China can be seen at regular intervals usually accompanied by the "Chen Guang". These special police wear dull green uniforms, and ride around in motorcycles with side cars. Their main job is to police the sidewalks, discouraging peddlers and other illegal sidewalk activities.

The traffic assistants are posted at intersections. They are elderly volunteers, armed with red armbands, flags and whistles. They tell you when to stop and go. When in doubt just watch their hand gestures. You will know that you shouldn't have run that red light by hearing a shrill whistle blowing and shouting behind you.

Alcohol & Bikes don't mix:

Here is a nickel's worth of free advice. I know that most of you adventurers who are reading this book are young, or young at heart to say the least. Try not to drink and ride, even though the night spots in China are legendary, and you will want to stay out till the crack of dawn. After seeing and hearing what happened to some of my acquaintances, it's better just to call a taxi for the ride home. The taxi drivers are usually happy to throw your bicycle in the trunk; it's safe there even if it's hanging halfway out.

It's rather interesting to note that we western folk don't usually associate drinking with riding a bicycle. This is because the last time most of us rode a bicycle for transportation, we were-15-years old! Still, it can be a dangerous reality while riding the crowded and chaotic streets of China's cities, and you need all your senses and wits about you.

Bottlenecks

Bottlenecks are an all too common occurrence when a lot of people or vehicles are trying to go somewhere. While riding in China you will get stuck in bottlenecks from time to time. Instead of yelling "why they don't build wider roads"!, or cursing out your fellow commuters, I recommend that you simply get off your bicycle and walk around it if possible. Sometimes it's what you have to do.

In Conclusion

The Ballet of Chaos never ceases to amaze me. I would spend hours some days on my balcony, sitting in a lawn chair, cold beer in hand, and just watch the traffic all moving in an almost synchronized fashion. Trucks and buses hogging the center stage, taxis and cars weaving around the bigger vehicles, and finally the humble bicycles and san lun ches dodging and maneuvering out of everyone else's way. The bicycles always reminded me of a large school of fish, staying as close as possible for protection from the bigger predators. This is the Ballet of Chaos; it holds me in awe, something dangerous and also to be respected. As a new denizen in China you must find your place in it, learn from it, ride in it, and ultimately conquer and enjoy it. Chapter 8 deals with a moment that comes to us all, (besides death and taxes). That moment is, when your bike is stolen.

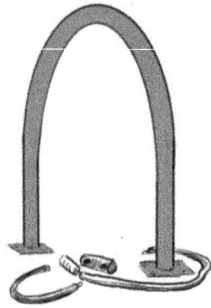

CHAPTER 8

"WHEN YOUR BIKE IS STOLEN"

Thievery exists in every country, China being no exception to this rule. Granted, China is one of the safer countries for ex-pats to live in, but oh crime does exist, mostly in the form of thievery. Bicycle theft is probably the most common form of crime you will come across during your stay.

It's really an unpleasant feeling that you get when one morning you wake up, have breakfast, dress and head down stairs only to find out your bike isn't where it should be! In fact it's nowhere to be seen! It's been ripped off, stolen, nicked, swiped, filched, rifled, seized, and pinched (被偷了, bei tou le).

As far as feelings in this kind of situation go, I find that at first I feel panicked and look around hoping on the off chance that I might see my bike. Then comes the sour realization that I've been had, followed by the fury, rage, and all the self righteous indignation I can muster. Finally, you just feel violated and sad.

How could such a thing happen? Well, as I've said before, your bike getting stolen in China is just a formality. It will happen. I personally would be very surprised if you lived there one or two years and still had the same bike. If you do manage to pull that off, please let me know, and I'll make up some kind of reward and mail it to you. Now, let's take a brief look at these shadowy people who are the cause of all this mischief.

About Thieves or "Shao Tou"

I have seldom seen them; any thief is worth his salt, if he is quick and invisible. The only thieves I saw during my stay in China where those who were caught in the act, or spotted before they could act and they fled. Also they seldom work alone, usually in groups. How many? Who can say? Pertaining to bike thieves, they seem to be fairly well organized. I will go into this in the following sections.

Running Thieves

I have observed these thieves only once or twice, but, in my opinion they are probably the gutsiest of them. What these guys do is stand around on street corners waiting for a school of bicycles to come by.

Once said school comes by, these thieves look for women, or anyone, with an open book bag or purse. Once the victim is acquired, the thieves begin to jog along behind the unsuspecting bicyclist. Trying to match their speed with that of the cyclist, then they put their hand in the bag and grab whatever they can, then run into a nearby alley. Most of the time, the person who has been robbed usually doesn't realize it until arriving at his or her destination.

The incident I witnessed was foiled due to a good Chinese citizen who was riding behind a lady who was about to get pick-pocketed. He noticed the thief and began to shout, the lady turned around and the thief panicked and ran. So always keep your purses and pocket books zipped and buttoned up. Keep them where you can see them and keep looking over your shoulder from time to time.

Drive by Thieves

So you have placed your lock on your bike, it's all nice and secure, or so you thought. But, not from the drive-by thieves, who usually own a san lun che or small truck. They work in gangs. While one group scouts out the street, the others follow in a truck. These rogues don't fool around. They will actually lift whole bikes up and throw them into the back of the truck like a sack of potatoes.

Once they have acquired a decent haul of bikes, they hightail it down some side streets to make good their escape. Sometimes they are caught red-handed by the police and a chase that would make the "Dukes of Hazard" jealous ensues. There is little you can do to thwart this kind of crime except secure your bicycle to something immobile; or if you are with a friend chain your bikes together to make them heavier and more awkward to lift.

How the police can help

Well, in most cases they can't. By no means do I mean the police are incompetent, they are simply overwhelmed by all the other kinds of crime found in large cities. Bicycle theft is so common in takes the lower rungs of the ladder in terms of urgency.

Still, don't give up hope. About 90% of the time when you bike gets stolen it's gone, boohoo, get over it and buy another expendable one. It's like dropping your car keys into a pool of molten lava. Don't reach after them, because they are gone.

I did mention that 90% not 100% so there still is a small chance your bike could have been recovered by the police and is urgently waiting for you to come liberate it. You see, all bikes in China are issued with a license number, much like automobiles. Be sure to write yours down in case the worst occurs. That way if you are really attached to your bike, you can go to the police station and let them know.

If memory serves, one of my good friends had his bike stolen, and being rather fond of the bike he went to the police station, jumped through the bureaucratic hoops, filled out all the forms. Six months later he receives a phone call from the police: they have found his bike. He goes to the impounding yard, and what a big place it was-about 200 yards of bicycles, cars, other assorted items. The officer took him over to a giant warehouse and opened the massive door. The inside was very similar to the warehouse at the end of the "Raiders of the Lost Ark" movie. It was enormous, no end in sight! There were just rows and rows of rusty cobwebby bicycles, motor scooters, E-bikes, etc. It seemed as if many would never see their former masters or the light of day again.

My friend found his bicycle none the worse for wear. It was just a little dusty and scratched, but other than that it was fine. The moral of this story is that yes, miracles do happen, but expect the worst.

Holidays

The time of year can have a profound effect on the levels of bicycle theft in China's cities. During the holiday seasons when many of the citizens of the cities go back home to visit family, bikes get stolen. I was never quite sure why this is so. Some of my Chinese friends explained to me that the farmer-workers steal the bikes to go home. I have been puzzled by this, because some of them live very far away-so far that it might take as much as a week or so of riding to get home. Anyway, I digress; the point is to be extra vigilant of your bicycle around holiday seasons. The Moon Festival usually falls around the end of September to early October; and the Spring Festival, which falls around the end of January to early February. The exact times change every year, depending on the lunar calendar.

Conclusion

These are all the methods and ways of the thief that I have learned during my time in China. Also what I deemed to be useful regarding locks, camouflage, security and so forth. I said it before and I will say it again: "A little bit of paranoia goes a long way." Don't be afraid to be paranoid about where you store your bicycle or even glance out of the restaurant window every now and again. It may save your bike.

In the event your bicycle is stolen, my advice would be the "Three Gets": 1) get mad, 2) get over it, 3) get another bike. That's the pattern all ex-pats have adopted. I think you will learn from each successive theft; at least, you're not likely to repeat the same mistake as before. Speaking of the ex-pat ways, the next chapter will share some stories and misadventures that I and my fellow ex-pats have had on the streets in China.

CHAPTER 9

"EX-PAT TALES OF CONCRETE AND ASPHALT"

Expatriates, or "Ex-pats" as we are fond of calling ourselves, are the travelers from many foreign lands who take up residence in a strange country for several months to several years. During such times we gather many stories. The stories are pooled together on weekend nights down at the local watering hole, or perhaps they travel by word of mouth, or the "bamboo telegraph" as we like to call it.

Some of my favorite tales from my ex-pat friends were of their bicycle travels. I enjoyed hearing about mishaps, near-misses, near-hits, new/old bicycles both bought and stolen, bicycles that refused to quit, and ones that broke almost instantly.

No matter what the story was or who told it, we all sympathized or laughed with the storyteller. We did this because we were all in the same boat; your bike was essentially your car, and a large part of one's daily life while residing in China. The short anecdotes that follow are just a small sampling of the vast ocean of stories that I heard or experienced during my stay.

Tale # 1 "Chipped"

Dave, Washington, USA

(Note, Dave's story concern's me as well, as I was a party to the following incident.)

Dave was a cautious man; he always wore a helmet. This might be the norm in many western nations; however, it turns heads in China. Many of my friends and I never wore them, so I suppose in a terrible way it was rather ironic what happened that day.

The three of us were riding cross town to a friend's house. We were playing it safe, cruising at a slow speed in the bicycle lane. We were riding in a "V" formation. Dave was the center; I was on the right wing, John on the left.

The place we were travelling to was well known to John and me. Dave however, had never been there before. This is where the trouble began. The entrance to the apartment complex was really just a narrow alley. John and I knew where and when to turn; we wrongly assumed David knew this as well. John and I both turned right on cue, Dave continued straight ahead, and then it happened.

John's front tire smashed into Dave's front tire knocking Dave off balance. Dave crashed to the ground, going down face first. I continued for one or two seconds before realizing what had happened. I quickly dismounted and sprinted back to the scene of the collision. Dave was getting up and cussing up a storm. I immediately realized why. He looked as if Mike Tyson had given him a left hook to his face, shattering his two front teeth. Dave asked me to inspect his teeth; I said his front teeth were chipped pretty badly. "I could feel my teeth grinding against the asphalt," Dave managed to spit out.

John came over, apologizing profusely, and then we started looking for Dave's teeth fragments. That absurd children's song "All I want for Christmas is my two front teeth" kept popping into my head the whole time. We managed to find some of the fragments. It was difficult because of other bicycle traffic. The pieces we did find, I put into a small plastic bag for safekeeping.

After that we walked our bikes to the apartment. John managed to wave down a taxi, and the three of us rode across town to a foreign-staffed hospital. (Some cities have hospitals staffed with western doctors). These places come in handy if you don't speak the language, granted you have to find them first. Well, long story short, we got Dave to the hospital, they fixed his teeth up good, and now he has a million dollar smile again.

What I learned:

I learned two very important lessons from this. First, make sure that everyone in your riding party knows the final destination. If they don't know, make sure that everyone gets a heads-up before a turn or a shortcut you might have in mind. Don't ever assume (like we did) that everyone knows where and when to turn.

Second, when falling off your bike, fight your natural instinct to put your arms out in front of you to break your fall. Usually your arms are too weak to stop the force of your fall. Instead wrap your arms around your head and face. That's where all the important stuff is!

Tale # 2   "Make mine pink, with polka dots please!"

Chris, Somerset, U.K. and John, California, USA.

My second tale takes place during the summer of my third year in China. Over the previous year I had become quite good friends with several other ex-pats. Two of them stand out in particular in regards to this tale.

Chris was from England. He was tall, lanky, and intelligent. He had spent some time overseas before in Madagascar doing biology work, his specialty was the lemur. We would always trade stories back and forth about our various experiences, his in Madagascar, and mine in Romania. Chris had a ridiculously bad sense of direction. I remember he would tape a GPS device to his bicycle's handlebars, just to find his way around the city. But for this eccentricity he was probably one of the kindest and most gentle friends I've ever had.

If I could use one word to describe John, it would be "Mirth". Come to think of it, we really don't use that word much in the English language today.

Definition: Mirth (**noun**)

1. gaiety or jollity, especially when accompanied by laughter: *the excitement and mirth of the holiday season.*

But that was John, he was filled with mirth, and goodwill toward his fellowman. Now John was what we call an "ABC" or American Born Chinese. From head to toe he looked very much like a local of Hangzhou. His outward features only served to disguise the fact that he spoke no Chinese upon his arrival in China. You see, John's great, great, great grandfather immigrated to California during the gold rush of 1849.

Like so many others he found no gold, but proceeded to make a living by other means. His family had lived in America since 1849, and everyone in his family had married other Chinese-Americans. John recalled even his grandfather spoke only a word or two of Chinese. However, I'm getting a bit off track, back to the story.

So one day Chris and I decided to play a practical joke on John. After all who would appreciate a good practical joke more than "Mr. Mirth" himself? So Chris and I set down to thinking. We thought of all the old classics, whoopee cushion, prank calls, etc. We ended up ruling them all out due to cost or difficulty. Then we started chatting about our bikes.

For a middle/lower class ex-pat, your bike defines your character a great deal. It is a source of pride, a tool, a trademark, it can also be a cause for shame our ridicule. Bearing the latter in mind, Chris and I began to concoct a plan.

John rode a nice bike. It was a nice bike indeed, a real 10-speed, very fast and beautiful, to look at. Therefore we decided we had to deface it. Yes, it seems mean. With friends like us, who needs enemies, right? On a positive note, doing this would cut down on the chances of his nice beautiful bike being stolen. See? Overseas you always help your friends out. Even when playing a practical joke on them.

John would always park his bike under the stairwell of the apartment block he inhabited. Those of you readers who have already been to China know what I'm talking about. It is customary for several families who live in these flats or apartments to cram all their bicycles under the stairs on the ground floor. It is difficult to see which bike is yours at nighttime as there is usually only one forlorn light bulb hanging from the ceiling.

Taking this into account, Chris and I stopped at the local hardware kiosk;

and bought two cans of spray paint, one pink and the other white. We arrived at John's flat a little after sundown. After some quiet rummaging we managed to pull John's 10 speed out, and proceeded to spray the body pink, and then add white dots here and there. At one point we were having trouble controlling ourselves and thought we might have to leave early for fear of waking the tenants. Having finished, we stepped back and admired our work. It looked like a new bicycle, or at least a completely different one. After another chuckle or two, we placed the bike back in its spot under the stairs.

About an hour or so later we called John from a teahouse in downtown Hangzhou and innocently asked if he wanted to come hang out. John said sure, and that he would be right over. Long story short, John walked past that bike about five times looking for his bike in the gloomy bike storage area. He was sure it had been stolen, and when he finally found out, well, I will leave the rest up to your speculation. It wasn't so bad. He thought it was a good joke and started talking to us again after a week or so.

Tale # 3   "Sabotage"

Betty, Hangzhou P.R.C

Riding at nighttime in China's cities was always a memorable experience. You see it's quite different from riding in western cities after night has fallen. First off, the streets are well lit, really bright street lamps shine from above, as well as neon signs, creating a funky Vegas strip feel. There are also scores of people out and about. The Chinese cities don't close down until very late in the evening. If you're riding around the city center, chances are you will have plenty of kindred spirits to accompany your travels.

It was one such night that my future wife (although, I didn't know it at the time) and I were riding back from a date. We were cruising along with a small group of strangers, not a care in the world, when all of a sudden my future wife and the rest of the pack dropped behind me. All the while I continued to talk to the air.

I pull on the brakes and look behind me. My wife and about four other Chinese people are cursing and looking disgustedly at their very flat tires. Now, I'm not the sharpest knife in the drawer, and I've had a flat before, but never had I seen multiple flats in one patch of roadway.

Upon further inspection (which proved difficult in the dark) I found no holes in my wife's tires. Then I noticed a small glint on the pavement, it sparkled dully in the faint glow of the street light. I picked it up; on closer inspection I saw it for what it was. It resembled a flachette; but was nothing more than a bicycle spoke, filed down to a sharp point and clipped about 1/8 of an inch long. There must have been several dozen scattered around the bike lane in this one area.

I held the caltrop up to the light for the rest of the group to see. They began to mutter and curse, and then they stormed off down the street walking their bikes. My wife followed them; I decided to walk my bike, too, because I didn't know how many more of these things might be scattered about.

On the way up the street, my wife explained to me that this "sabotage" is a fairly common occurrence. It is perpetrated by some unscrupulous bike repair vendors, in order to drum up extra business. They ride along at night, tossing nails, tacks, or these specially-made bikes' spokes out onto the bike lanes at intervals of a minute or so. Then set up shop down the street and wait for the business to come.

Where's the justice, I thought?   There would be justice tonight, mob justice that is.   The crowd was getting more and more angry by the minute, and then they saw the alleged culprits' with the shop set up by the next intersection.

The ensuing argument was loud and animated, to say the least. I thought they were going to fall upon the repair men and rip them to shreds.   Both were young men, rather dirty and unkempt, most likely from the countryside. Desperation was their game, sinking so low just to make 10 cents from a tire repair.   The feelings of the victims were obvious, my own were more ambiguous.   I was angry at what they had done, but it was really just pathetic.

I couldn't help but feel slightly sorry for them.   What would push them to be so petty, so underhanded?   Just for a small sum, and most likely no return business!   My thoughts were interrupted by a shrill police whistle. The two men bolted down the street and into the dark, followed by the taunts and threats of the crowd.   My wife and I quietly slipped away down a side street.   I dislike crowds at the best of times.

Tale # 4   "Nicknames and Superstitions"

Ex-pats, Hangzhou, P.R.C

This tale is devoted to the quirkiness that tended to affect a lot of us ex-pats who lived in China; especially those of us who were avid bike riders. As I mentioned earlier we grew attached to our bikes, even gave them names.   One of my friends from Mexico rode a bright yellow mountain bike which he affectionately dubbed "La Bamba".

I often referred to my third bicycle as "The Beast". This unaffectionate nickname was earned due to my bike's awkward nature and unusually heavy weight. I never found out how much the bike did weigh but it was so heavy it was difficult to move up steps and over curbs. I always had to pedal twice as hard to keep up with companions who possessed bikes with aluminum frames.

For others, there were even little rituals and superstitions that took hold over the days, weeks, and months of riding in the daily commute. Sometimes these developed slowly and unobtrusively. Other times they came about after a near miss in traffic, or some other traumatic event. An Irish man from Dublin; always crossed himself and muttered a quick prayer before heading out into traffic for the day. This was a ritual that I was totally in agreement with.

Still others would mark their bikes for various reasons. Some ex-pats would paint slash marks on the jock bars of the bicycles, maybe to show how many years they had been in country. Or perhaps how many accidents they had walked away from, how many bikes had been stolen from them. I thought of adorning my bicycle with painted symbols, but quickly rejected the idea as it most likely would have attracted thieves. That was about as close to "nose art" that any of us ever came to.

With E-bikes and motor scooters it was different. Because of all the plastic cowling, you could put stickers or symbols up; the national flag of the rider was often a popular choice. If you are planning to put stickers on your bike, it's unlikely you could find them in China; better to buy them at home and bring them over. But, remember, they will make your bike more conspicuous, increasing the chances that it might get stolen.

One man's bike will always remain in my mind; I think he was a gentleman from Jamaica. Instead of reflectors on his bike, he had CD's, which did the job admirably. You could see him coming down the street a long way off at nighttime. Flashing ultraviolet wheels spinning round and round. He definitely wins the award for foreigner turning the most heads.

My five years in country I witnessed many strange events, people's pet peeves, superstitions, adornments, all associated with their bikes. Your bicycle will take on a character all its own, and who knows? Perhaps you will develop your own little rituals, superstitions and adornments. I hope so. At least, it will make your time there certainly more memorable. And please remember to take some pictures.

CHAPTER 10

"THE BEST WAY TO EXPERIENCE CHINA"

One day not too long ago, a friend and I were having lunch at a diner, one of those little greasy spoon types of places. You know the kind were all the locals go to get the best sandwiches, well certainly the greasiest, anyway.

Over lunch the subject of China came up and he asked me what my most enjoyable experience over there had been. "Traveling around Hangzhou by bicycle," I replied. My friend's face betrayed his mild surprise. Perhaps he was expecting a more "cultural" response (while mind you the bicycle is very much forever locked in its own place in Chinese culture).

Oh, there are many other experiences that I enjoyed while in China; and it's my dearest wish that you, the reader and future traveler, can enjoy them, too. Having tea in one of the older tea houses around the famous West Lake, with one arm out the window, the lake view slightly obscured by the lazy branches of the willow trees. Watching as the populace slowly drifts by, apparently oblivious to your presence, all the while sipping the world famous Dragon Well green tea from a shallow porcelain cup.

Another memory that I often dwell upon was taking long walks through the bamboo forests that surround the city. A very peculiar noise occurs when the wind whips through the leaves of a bamboo forest. It's a creaking and groaning noise. It's rather unsettling if you are alone, or at least I found it to be. I would go into these bamboo forests in search of bamboo shoots. This young bamboo can be cut out of the earth, taken back home, cooked and eaten. The Chinese showed me how to do this and I began these excursions by myself after a short while.

The bicycle is hands down the best way to see China and her people. It is probably the most rewarding way to traverse a city in China. I mean this in the sense of capturing the pure ambiance of the culture, the sights, sounds, smells, the danger, excitement. It's also best from a very practical standpoint of course: traffic jams and parking hardly affect you at all. Even the inexpensive, reliable bus is not as mobile as your trusty bike. The bus stays on its set route, gets stopped in traffic and frequently stops to let people on and off. But on your bike, you go wherever you want to.

Master of the Alleys

After several days of riding around your city, you will begin to seek out short-cuts to get to work or friends' apartments. Alleys frequently provide ideal shortcuts. Some alleys are only wide enough to accommodate a single bicycle while others are broad enough to drive a car down them with ease. These alleys, called "Hutongs" in Beijing, give a unique look at the lives of many of the denizens of a Chinese city.

Imagine you are riding down the street and passed by the entrance to one of these alleys. The noonday sun is hot, and the alley's coolness beckons you, although not much is visible in the dim twilight-like darkness inside. After a moment's hesitation, you turn your bike and plunge in.

You pick up a burst of speed from the decline down from the street. The alley is cool as it promised to be, the ground is uneven and broken, and you have to deftly maneuver around some debris in the road. Once you gain a sense of this, you begin to look around.

While riding by, it's fascinating to see how people have ingeniously used the limited space. A carefully tended garden is neatly tucked into a small courtyard not bigger than a bedroom. A cat easily squeezes through the bars of a chipped and rusted green iron fence, of the kind typical of each dwelling. It is startled by your noisy approach and scurries behind some miniature lemon trees and other plants. The right side of the alley is made up of an old mortar and brick wall, many patches are in disrepair, the bricks are old and worm eaten, some have fallen onto the sides of the alley.

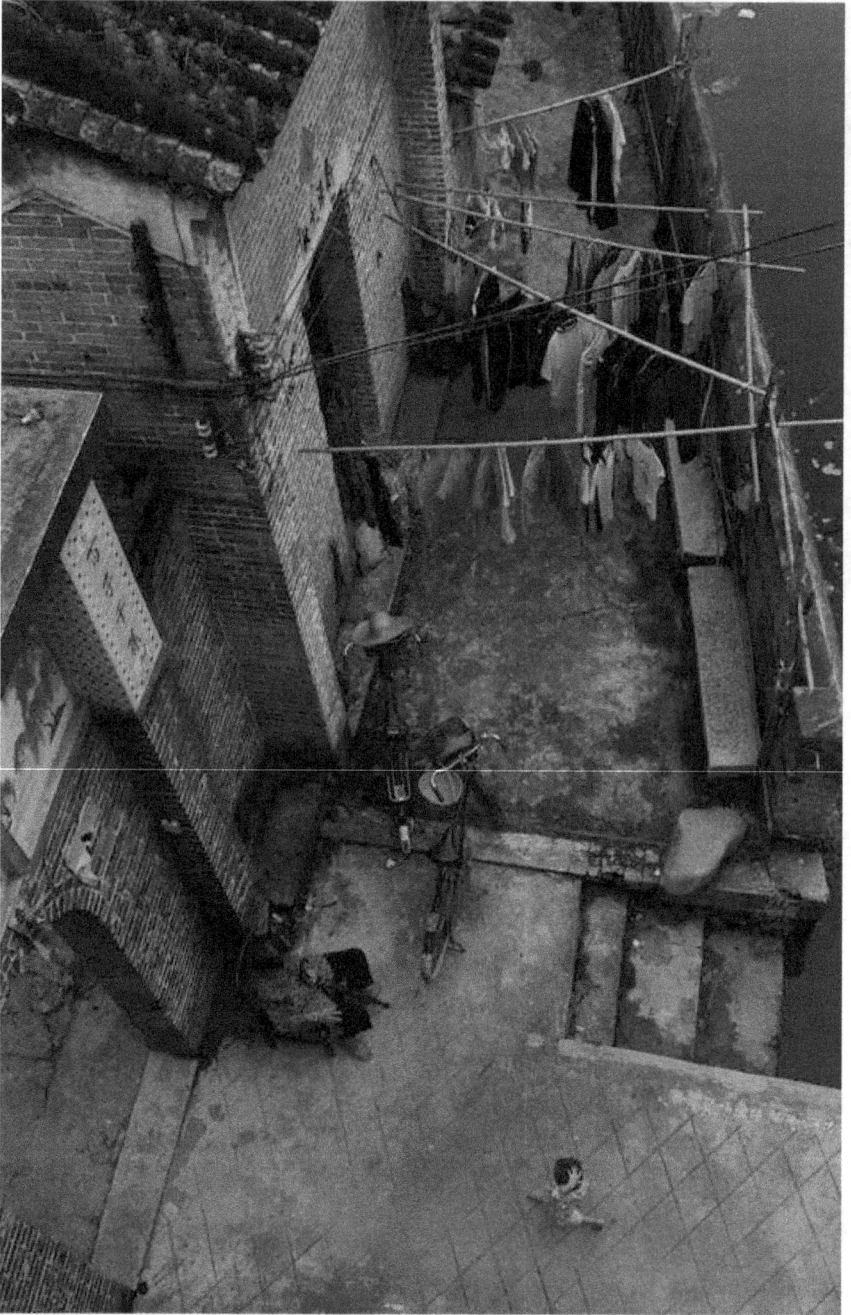

You finally emerge from the alley. The sun temporarily blinds you, but it is

less strong here. Where is here anyway? You are in a small residential area, a miniature version of the city. As you look around you see an old road paved with rockcrete. Both sides are lined with trees, and behind them are apartment blocks.

In addition to this, there are people everywhere. Children move in groups down the street, happily chatting, and going into one of the small convenience stores to get ice cream. You pedal out into the bustling thoroughfare. You hear snippets of conversations you don't understand, the people speaking so quickly and in dialect.

Off to your right you catch a glimpse of two old men, still sporting their "Mao suits" and arguing over something, perhaps their game of Chinese chess. A new group of people come toward you. Their uniform clothing makes you think for a moment that another school had gotten out, but then you see their faces, too old for students; only factory workers wear these types of uniforms. They crowd into the sidewalk noodle kitchens, eager for dinner. You begin to feel slightly dizzy, as you are not used to this much social activity around you. You are torn between wanting to escape the cacophony or jump into it, to be a part of something much bigger than yourself.

Pedaling down the street you look for the alley that led you to this place; trying to escape the incredible hustle and bustle around you. The numerous alleys seem as one and it becomes an impossibility to locate the one you came in through. You begin to realize that you are lost. Directions could be asked, but the language barrier would prove difficult and you have barely memorized the name of your school or the hotel where you are staying.

You are struck by the absurdness of your situation; now what am I supposed to do? Ride around forever!? I could get even more lost, or perhaps I can wait until the sun goes down, then at the very least I will know which way is west. Maybe I can keep asking people if any one speaks English, it will be like playing the lottery, maybe I will get lucky. Judging from the amount of people in the streets the odds are pretty much the same as a lottery.

Continuing down the street, the neighborhood gives way to a main thoroughfare with bicycle lanes. You are not familiar with this section of the city though. It is mostly industrial. Full of factories, holding tanks, rusty pipes with old asbestos insulation hanging from them, gives the impression of giant old trees with Spanish moss hanging down and gently swaying in the breeze. Everything here is dusty, old and worn out looking. Many of the workers share the same look as the factories; they stare at you as you ride by. Some of the younger looking workers shout, "Hello!" to you.

Farther down the strip of old forlorn looking factories, you spot some brightly lit establishments: small apartment like dwellings lit with pink neon lights and in some cases Christmas tree lights. As you draw closer, you notice that these places are advertised as "massage" parlors. There seem to be an awful lot of these massage parlors around. Then the terrible truth of what they really are hits you. It all matches up, pretty girls wearing tight clothes, waiting patiently in a row near the front window. The workers going in, sometimes in groups, sometimes one at a time; it dawns on you that you have ridden into a red-light, or in this case "pink light," district of the city. In most countries this is usually a place you don't want to stroll through. You put the pedal to the metal and cruise on out of the pink light district just as the sun sets. You ride on farther into the city. A beautiful sunset paints the skyline bright oranges, reds, pinks, purples, and finally blues and grays. The first few stars begin to wink their lights. Simultaneously the street lights begin to hum to life, and the evening heart of the Chinese city begins to beat.

And what a heart it is, too, bustling crowds going shopping, all manner of peddlers on the sidewalks, one eye on potential customers, the other on the lookout for the chungguang or sidewalk police. You pull over to the side of the bike lane, finding that you have worked up quite an appetite, being lost and all. A middle-aged man is selling some sort of dumpling soup from a small shop built into the side of a building. The small enterprise sports three folding tables arranged on the sidewalk, with folding stools. Each table has a bottle with dark vinegar, and a plastic squeeze bottle filled with some sort of chili sauce. You sit down at the table, he sees you and shuffles over, then is taken back when he notices your foreign features. He promptly says, "Hello!" in a loud and heavily accented voice. He chatters away happily about something and gives you a menu. Hmm...It's all in Chinese characters. Well, you've only been in country a few days and decide to be adventuresome; you close your eyes and point to one. He nods happily and goes back into his little kitchen.

While you wait, your gaze shifts over to the street and the bike lanes, an indescribable mix of people passes by constantly- a murmuring, chattering, arguing, laughing, river of humanity. You are brought back from your thoughts by the cook, as he cheerfully places in front of your some form of soup noodles. Struggling with the chopsticks you manage to get the noodles into your mouth. They taste delicious. But, they are rather salty and you reach for the plastic cup of water for a drink. It is flimsy and the water almost scalds you. It's rather strange, but you understand the logic of everyone drinking boiled tap water; still, you miss your ice cubes.

CITY CENTER

After dinner you pay and wave goodbye to the cook. Once again you mount up and try to orient yourself, judging by the size of the buildings you must be near the center of the city. The city seems to be one of great contrasts: a place where poverty and prosperity, princes and paupers, traditional and contemporary all live side by side; perhaps not all in harmony with one another, but in the closest of proximities. As you ride across the downtown strip, you glance at all the legitimate as well as knockoff businesses, Tommy Hilinger, Eastface, Mike, Naturally JoJo, etc. You chuckle and know the names will stay with you for quite some time to come. The West certainly has had its influence here: KFC's, McDonalds, Haagen-Dazs, Papa Johns, Pizza huts; the list goes on and on. Even the most nauseating symbol of capitalism, Hooters, makes a surprise appearance at the end of the street. The Best Western and Hyatt hotels take their rightful places on the cityscape skyline.

Still, down below, on street level, the old China asserts itself, with you caught in the middle. You cruise by a park from which loud waltz music is blaring. There are about 20 older couples slow dancing to this music. Across from this display, some youths ride skateboards near a fountain, practicing their jumps and slides. You find that you are constantly being distracted from finding your way home. There is just so much to take in. Quite frankly, its sensory overload, you notice another darkened alley, your curiosity gets the better of you. Be prepared to be distracted again.

NIGHT MARKET

A brightly lit alleyway beckons. Old carnival style light bulbs are strung out between stalls and stretch down the alley as far as you can see. While the hour grows late, you decide that this needs to be checked out. After carefully crossing the busy street you see the night market up close. Vendors stretch back into the darkness; voices and shouts intermingle, and then are lost in some auto recording blaring out its message repeatedly. Perhaps it's broadcasting the best deals in town. Immediately you realize that you will have to walk as it's a narrow fit between the tables, not to mention the crush of people. Walking the bike through is probably the best course of action, as it's safe in your hands, and you don't need to go back for it.

The first several tables are filled with knockoff products; everything from North Face jackets to Rolex watches that look practically real. Many of the vendors watch impassively as you slowly walk by. Some smile and others beckon you to look at their wares. The tables in the middle of the alley interest you the most. They are piled high with baubles, mementos, and images of China's recent past. Gazing at the table you view stacks of old posters from the 1920's and 30's, a time known for its corruption and decadence: smiling Chinese women dressed in bright silk Chi-paos selling Camel Cigarettes, soap, and cruise tickets for the Shanghai/Frisco line. A few inches over, there is a pile of old KMT metals, pins, and awards. The white sun with 12 rays is faded now, a former shadow of its past glory as the first republic of China. Looking upon his lost revolution is a portrait of Sun Yat-sen, the first president of China.

The other half of the table varies from the first; much like the second half of the 20th century was different from the first for China. Red pennants and little red books are piled up there. Little busts of Chairman Mao Zedong adorn the table. It's a time of totalitarian "Cultricide" and anarchy. Madness and hatred prevailed. The past of this country that you are visiting both intrigues and worries; you decide to make it a point to study it more later on.

There is also a food section in this night market. They sell everything from candied apples to noodles. The food vendors do not strike you as being from the city, as they look different, wearing homemade gold earrings and worn-out clothes. There are even some Uighur people (Ethnic Muslims from Xinjiang) selling their famed nut cakes from the back of their trikes, or san lun ches. They are clearly not Han Chinese as their faces resemble more central Asian peoples. You are now approaching the end of the alley. There are a few more tables with pets and old Buddha statues on them. A motorcycle and sidecar are parked at the end of the alley. The Chen Guang are apparently looking for both thieves and unlicensed vendors.

HOME COMING

As you pass the final glowing carnival bulb, darkness envelopes the alley again, the crowd thins out. The only real light is the gentle glow of a neon green sign for a noodle restaurant. Getting back on your bike, you pedal faster down the remainder of the alley and out onto a major street. The traffic on the streets has lessened considerably since the daytime. Now you can ride at speed and deftly maneuver around the slower san lun ches and people walking in the bike lane. The night breeze is cool, you find yourself really enjoying this experience, even if you are lost. You wonder how often people in your home country have done something like this in their entire lives? Then you suddenly see something on the horizon. A tall brightly lit strange shaped building. Excitement builds in you as you immediately recognize the building. Suddenly you know which direction leads the way back to your apartment. That building is right next to where you live! Taking a right at the next intersection you pedal briskly towards your home away from home. After about a half hour of hard riding you finally return. You dismount and carefully lock your bike up in the shed outside the apartment building. You give the bicycle and affectionate pat before you leave it, "My faithful steed" you joke to yourself. You do find that you have taken a strange liking to the bike.

REFLECTIONS

Later in your apartment, drinking some tea, you reflect on the day's events. You've experienced a great deal of this city today. You think about all the different parts of the city there are, from run down factory districts to glittering skyscrapers to shadowy night markets. This tour of the city didn't cost you a dime and you have learned so much. Before turning in for the night you decide to head out again tomorrow, this time with a compass or GPS....nah, perhaps being lost is what made it such an interesting day.

END OF THE LINE

I wrote this short story to give the reader some idea of the typical day on a bike in a major city of China.   Getting lost- while I don't recommend it if you're a fresh fish in a foreign land- is actually one of the better ways to get acquainted with the culture and its people.   Not that I would get lost on purpose, but I found that my curiosity always got the better of me during my early months in China.   I just had to see where this alley went, or that lane led. And while you are exploring the streets, you always manage to taste the local cuisine, drink bubble milk tea, and converse with the locals.   Most of them are quite friendly and curious about foreigners. This book is intended to make you more aware of what dangers/wonders await you, the traveler, tourist, businessman and teacher that comes to live in this strange land. I honestly wish I had some of this foresight/information before I had journeyed to China.

So now I have passed on all I know and experienced during my five years in the bicycle lanes of China. You have a preference for a certain style of bike floating in your head already, I'm sure. You know how to safeguard your bike from the ever-present thief, make rudimentary repairs to ensure that you get to your destination, how to ride in the night and adverse weather conditions, and how to survive rush hour; all that is left for you to do is to get out there and do it! Good luck to you, enjoy your biking experience and who knows, maybe someday we will meet on opposite sides of the Thin White Line.

EPILOGUE

Quincy, MA. USA.   Oct. 15th 2010

Gazing out the window at a typical New England autumn, I find I'm in one of my nostalgic moods. I've been home almost one year; it feels strange sometimes, like I've only been away a day or two. The diner I'm taking my breakfast in buzzes with the conversation and chatter of local people, about local thoughts, politics, and problems, all of it just terribly local. They can't help it, it's all people know who stay in one area for a long time. It's the curse of static living. I have the other curse, the worse one.

As I sip my coffee and gaze out at the changing leaves, I reflect on my condition. It's a very personal one, but is shared by others. Of whom do I speak? Why other ex-pats of course! What we share in common is that we all gave up normal lives or postponed them in our native lands. We chose to travel instead. We experienced the world and what it has to offer; we travelled farther than most people ever dream. Strange food and cultural difficulties were our constant companions. We were forever changed by these experiences, and the price we pay is that we can never return to the way we were before we left. We cease to be locals, in the true sense of the word. The curse I spoke of is mostly restlessness in our souls. We can never truly feel at home, because anywhere can be our home. It's a strange paradox that can affect you if you stray too far from your native land.

Dwelling on this condition, I notice an older Chinese man; he rides his bicycle up the street towards the diner. He wears an old wide -brimmed hat, to fend off the weakening autumn sun. His face is worn, leathery, betraying a lifetime of hard work and toil. He rides an old two speed bicycle, the paint is peeling off the body, and he has modified the bike greatly from its original form. Two plastic milk crates hang from each side; each holds plastic bags filled to the brim with soda cans. Another basket adorns the front of the bike.

As he rides by the diner he looks in my direction, for a brief instant our eyes lock. He is the American in China; I'm the Chinese in America. We are one and the same, we both have travelled thousands of miles from home, adapted to strange cultures, endured the different climate, food, the locals. We are so different yet the same. Our transportation was and is the bicycle. The moment passes, it's over.   The man glides by the diner; I look into my coffee, and then take another sip.   Much was left undone in China, my time there is over now.   I have to pick up the pieces and start anew in my native land.   I have to find out how to be a local again.

GLOSSARY

Bicycle	自行车 (zi xing che)
Wheel	轮子 (lun zi)
Seat	座椅 (zuo yi)
Oil	油 (you)
Chain	链条 (lian tiao)
How much?	多少钱？(duo shao qian)
Too Expensive	太贵了 (tai gui le)
Please/Thank you	麻烦你／谢谢 (ma fan ni/xie xie)
Thief	小偷 (xiao tou)
Stolen	被偷了 (bei tou le)
Repair/Fix	修车 (xiu che)
Broken	坏了 (huai le)
Basket	篮子 (lan zi)
Where is?	在哪儿？(zai na er)
Bell	铃 (ling)

www.ingramcontent.com/pod-product-compliance
Lightning Source LLC
Chambersburg PA
CBHW080545110426
42813CB00006B/1214